SCIENCE COOKERY

THROUGH

# Hot and Cold

**Peter Mellett**
**Jane Rossiter**

## FRANKLIN WATTS

New York • London • Toronto • Sydney

Franklin Watts, Inc.
95 Madison Avenue
New York, NY 10016

Library of Congress Cataloging-in-Publication Data

Mellett, Peter G., 1946-
    Hot and cold/by Peter Mellett and Jane Rossiter.
        p. cm. – (Science through cookery)
    Includes index.
    Summary: Examines the scientific principles of heat and cold
through the cooking of a variety of recipes from different countries
and cultures.
    ISBN 0–531–14236–1
1. Cookery–Juvenile literature. 2. Heat–Juvenile literature.
3. Cold–Juvenile literature. [1. Cookery. 2. Heat. 3. Cold.]
I. Rossiter. Jane. II. Title. III. Series.
TX652.5.M36 1993
536'.078–dc20                                                    92-5141
                                                                 CIP AC

**Senior editor:** Hazel Poole
**Series editor:** Jane Walker
**Designer:** Ann Samuel
**Illustrator:** Annabel Milne
**Photographer:** Michael Stannard
**Consultant:** Margaret Whalley

Additional photograph: p12, Simon
Fraser/Science Photo Library

The publisher would like to thank the
following children for their participation
in the photography of this book: Tom
Brownrigg, Caroline Rossiter, Alexander
Rossiter and Corinne Smith-Williams.

Typeset by Spectrum, London
Printed in Singapore

# Contents

# Introduction

**Science Through Cookery** is a new, simple and fun approach to learning about science. In each book you will not only read about science, but you will also have first-hand experience of real science. By linking science topics with simple cookery recipes, you can learn about science and at the same time cook some delicious recipes. Science is fun when you finish up eating the results of your work!

## About this book

In **Hot and Cold,** we look at the topic of heat energy, and its effects on different substances. **Hot and Cold** explains temperature and how it is measured, and investigates the various ways that heat can move from one place, or object, to another.

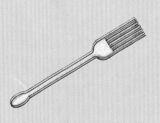

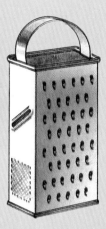

**Hot and Cold** explains important scientific principles with the help of clearly labeled diagrams and illustrations. The recipes offer a practical opportunity to gain a better understanding of the science you have just read about.

Each recipe has been carefully selected and written so that the cooking can be done with a minimum amount of adult supervision. Where the help of an adult is needed, for example when boiling a pan of water, this is clearly indicated.

The ingredients and equipment you will need are listed at the beginning of each recipe. They are easily obtainable and no special equipment is required. The step-by-step format of the recipes is easy to follow. Each step is illustrated with a photograph.

At the end of the book you will find a page of Further things to do. These are fun experiments and activities that are linked to many of the science concepts discussed in the book. A glossary of terms and an index are provided at the end of the book.

# Solid, liquid, or gas?

Everything in the world is either a solid, a liquid, or a gas. Solid substances are firm and do not change their shape. Liquids are runny and can be poured from one container to another. Gases are usually invisible and spread out to fill the space around them.

Every solid, liquid, and gas is made up from tiny invisible pieces called atoms. In most substances, the atoms are joined together in separate groups called molecules.

## Popsicles

### Ingredients
2 cups pure fruit juice, such as orange, pineapple, or apple juice

**Equipment**

a large measuring cup
a tablespoon
8 popsicle molds
8 wooden sticks
a plastic container

1 Place a stick in each popsicle mold.

2 Carefully pour the fruit juice into the cup and stir it well. Pour the juice into the molds, and put them in the freezer.

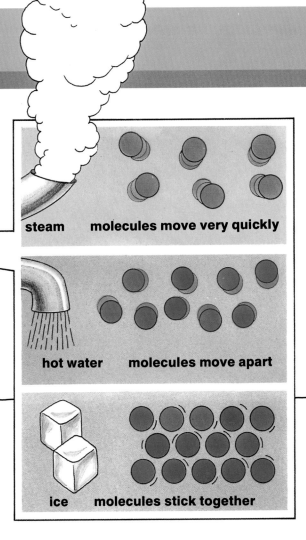

**steam**    **molecules move very quickly**

**hot water**    **molecules move apart**

**ice**    **molecules stick together**

Water is made from molecules that are all the same. The molecules in liquid water move about freely all the time. When water is heated, the molecules in it move faster. The hotter the water, the quicker the molecules move. The molecules in a lump of ice cling together firmly, but those in steam move so quickly that they escape completely from each other.

A single grain of sugar contains several million molecules of sugar. But the molecules in sugar and other solids, as well as in liquids and gases, are mostly empty space.

Imagine the molecules in a glass of water were made bigger so that they became the size of Ping-Pong balls. Each ball would be about 3 feet away from the next ball. In a cloud of steam, they would be over 3,000 feet from each other. Some water molecules in steam can travel as fast as the Concorde – about 1,600 miles per hour.

**3** After about 3 to 4 hours, the popsicles will be solid. Remove the popsicles from the molds, and store them in a container in the freezer.

# Melting

A popsicle is really a mixture of water and fruit juice which has been frozen into a solid. The molecules in a frozen popsicle cling together firmly. They move backward and forward as they gently vibrate.

But when you eat a popsicle in the hot sunshine, it soon starts to melt. A liquid drips from the popsicle. Why does this happen, and what are the molecules doing now? The heat from the sun makes the molecules inside the popsicle vibrate more quickly. Soon they move so fast that they break away from each other. The solid popsicle melts and turns into a liquid.

The word "chocolate" comes from an Aztec word meaning "cocoa water" or "bitter water." The Aztecs in Mexico made a chocolate drink by grinding cocoa beans, mixing them with water and spices, and heating the mixture to make a paste.

The paste was left to dry on leaves where it formed a solid block. The block was peeled off the leaf and mixed with hot water and maize to make a foaming hot chocolate drink.

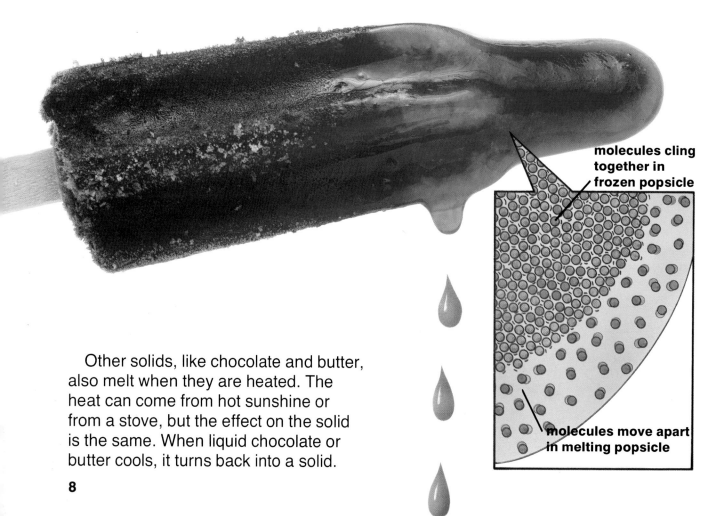

molecules cling together in frozen popsicle

molecules move apart in melting popsicle

Other solids, like chocolate and butter, also melt when they are heated. The heat can come from hot sunshine or from a stove, but the effect on the solid is the same. When liquid chocolate or butter cools, it turns back into a solid.

# Chocolate treats

## Ingredients
8oz plain chocolate

small fruits, such as grapes, pineapple chunks, strawberries, cherries, raisins, and dates

**Equipment**
a small glass bowl
a pot
a wooden spoon
toothpicks
wax paper

1 Break the chocolate into squares and put them into the bowl. Ask an adult to help you boil about 2 inches of water in a pot. Turn down the heat.

2 Gently place the bowl in the pot. Stir the chocolate until it melts. This takes about 3 to 5 minutes. Turn off the heat and take out the bowl.

3 Push a toothpick into a piece of fruit and dip the fruit into the melted chocolate. Place it on the wax paper until the chocolate hardens. Repeat with each fruit.

# Disappearing water

A wet cloth dries out slowly when it's left out in the sun. When you boil an egg, the water level in the pan goes steadily down. The hotter the water becomes, the quicker it seems to disappear.

The molecules in a liquid move around freely, bumping into each other all the time. Sometimes a molecule travels very fast because it has been hit by other molecules all at the same time. Fast-moving molecules escape completely from the surface of the liquid.

As molecules escape, the liquid slowly evaporates and becomes a gas or vapor. But when water boils, so many molecules escape so quickly that vapor forms inside the liquid, and not just at its surface. Bubbles rise to the surface and burst, releasing vapor into the air. Water evaporates from fresh fruit that is put out to dry in the sunshine. This is how grapes become raisins, and plums become prunes.

! The Tatars were a tribe of nomads who lived in Asia in the thirteenth century. They traveled long distances across the mountains, carrying all their food and drink supplies on horseback.

The Tatars dried the milk from their mares by leaving it in the sunshine. Water and dried milk were later placed in drinking bottles hung from the horsemen's saddles. The dried milk and water mixed to make liquid milk as the Tatars rode along.

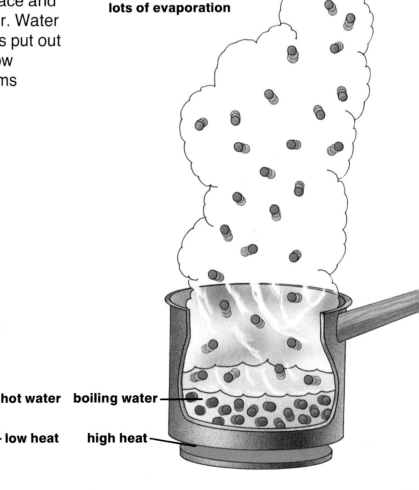

**lots of evaporation**

**some evaporation**

hot water

boiling water

low heat

high heat

# Tabbouleh

## Ingredients

3½ oz bulgar wheat
4 tablespoons fresh parsley
2 tablespoons fresh mint
2 tablespoons olive oil
6 scallions (green onions)

3 tomatoes
1 lemon
salt and pepper

## Equipment

2 large bowls
a knife
a cutting board
a grater
a lemon squeezer
a strainer
a tablespoon

**1** Put the bulgar wheat into a bowl and cover it with cold water. Leave it to soak for 20 minutes. The dried wheat swells as it soaks up water.

**2** Grate the yellow skin of the lemon (not the white inside of the rind). Cut the lemon in half and squeeze out the juice. Put the rind and juice in the bowl.

**3** Wash the parsley and mint, and chop finely. Wash the scallions and remove the outer leaves. Chop the tomatoes and onions. Add the chopped ingredients to the bowl.

**4** Drain the bulgar wheat and press out as much water as you can. Add it to the bowl, together with the oil, salt, and pepper. Mix well and serve.

# From a gas to a liquid

Drops of liquid water appear on the cold windows of a steamy kitchen. To find out where this water comes from, you must look back at the stove.

Water evaporates and escapes from hot food and pots of boiling water. The air in the kitchen fills with water vapor, which is water in the form of a gas. The molecules in this gas are moving very fast, and the gas quickly spreads throughout the kitchen.

Some molecules hit the cold windows. They make the windows slightly warmer, and this cools the water vapor. The molecules in the cooled water vapor move more slowly now. They have less energy. They move closer and stick together in small groups. These groups join up to make the drops of water on the windows. So heat evaporates water to make water vapor. Cooled water vapor condenses to make liquid water.

*When the warm air inside a room reaches the cold windows, the water vapor in the air cools and condenses to form drops of liquid water.*

# English steamed pudding

## Ingredients
2 tablespoons jelly
2 eggs
2 tablespoons milk
6oz self-rising flour
3½oz finely granulated sugar
3½oz soft margarine

**Equipment**
food scale
a large pot with a lid,
   or a steamer
an oven-proof glass or metal bowl
a tablespoon
a small bowl
a fork
a mixing bowl
a wooden spoon
aluminum foil and string

1 Half fill the pot with water and ask an adult to help you boil the water.

2 Grease the oven-proof bowl with a little margarine and put the jelly into the bottom of it.

3 Break the eggs into the small bowl. Add the milk and beat together well with a fork.

4 Put the flour, sugar, and margarine into the mixing bowl. Add the egg and milk mixture and combine all the ingredients with a wooden spoon.

5 Pour the mixture over the jelly in the bowl. Cover the top of the bowl with foil and tie a piece of string around it.

6 Ask an adult to stand the bowl in the boiling water or the steamer. Put on the lid and steam for 1½ hours. Add more water from time to time. Ask an adult to do this.

7 After 1½ hours, carefully remove the bowl from the pan or steamer. Take off the foil cover and turn the pudding out onto a plate.

# What is temperature?

**10,800°F**
surface of the sun

A cookbook tells you how hot your oven must be in order to cook different foods – very hot for baking cookies, but cooler for cooking meringues. The oven's temperature tells you how hot it is. Temperature is measured in degrees Fahrenheit, which is usually shortened to °F.

Ice freezes at 32°F, water boils at 212°F and cookies bake at about 350°-400°F. The temperature of a freezer is between −10°F and −5°F. The freezer is colder than melting ice.

**350°-400°F**

baking cookies

**300°F**

baking meringues

**212°F**

boiling an egg

**120°F**

the hottest desert

**32°F**

ice freezes

**−96°F**

the coldest place on Earth

**−460°F**
the lowest possible temperature – atoms and molecules stop moving

*This diagram shows some temperatures marked on the Fahrenheit scale, and some foods that cook at these temperatures.*

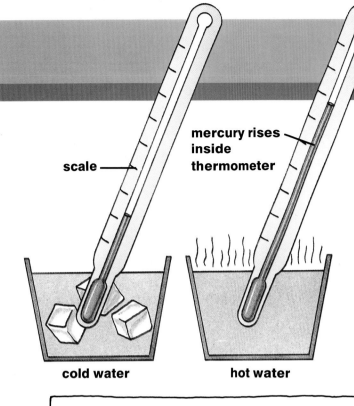

scale

mercury rises inside thermometer

cold water

hot water

You use temperature to say how hot or cold things are. You measure temperature with a thermometer. There are many different types of thermometers, but most people in the United States use the Fahrenheit scale to tell the temperature.

Glass thermometers contain a liquid, such as mercury or alcohol, inside a long, thin tube. The hotter the liquid inside the thermometer becomes, the more space it takes up. The liquid rises

# Deviled eggs

## Ingredients

4 eggs
2 oz cottage cheese
1 tablespoon mayonnaise
salt and pepper
paprika

**Equipment**

a pot
a small bowl
a knife
a teaspoon

a tablespoon
a fork
a cutting board

1 Place the eggs in the pot and cover with cold water. Ask an adult to help you bring the water to the boil. Boil the eggs for 10 minutes.

2 When the eggs are cooked, turn off the heat and carefully drain off the hot water. Run cold water onto the eggs until they feel cold.

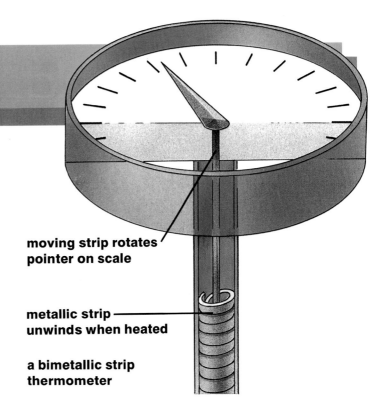

up inside the tube, which is marked with a temperature scale. Glass thermometers can accurately measure temperatures between 40°F to 572°F. But they are fragile and break easily.

Cooking thermometers are tougher but they are not so accurate. They contain strips of metal that bend as they heat up. The bending metal moves a pointer on a scale. Digital thermometers are accurate but can be expensive.

**moving strip rotates pointer on scale**

**metallic strip unwinds when heated**

**a bimetallic strip thermometer**

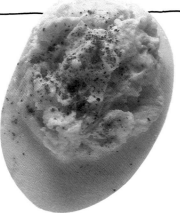

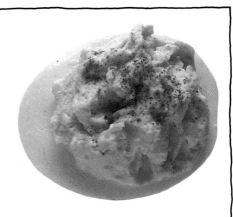

3 Remove the shells and cut the eggs in half lengthwise. Remove the yolks and use a fork to mash them in a bowl.

4 Add the cheese, mayonnaise, salt and pepper, and blend to a creamy mixture. Spoon the mixture into the egg halves and sprinkle with paprika.

# Freezing cold

When you put fresh raspberries in the freezer, they become hard. The water inside the fruit freezes as it changes from a liquid to a solid. All the molecules in the raspberries slow down as the freezer takes away warmth from the fruit. The water molecules in the raspberries no longer move freely past each other. Instead, they join together in groups which make up crystals of ice.

Ice crystals take up more room than the liquid water that made them. Raspberries are made up from tiny bags called cells. Each cell has a thin wall. These walls burst when the water inside expands as the ice forms. So when you take frozen raspberries out of the freezer and leave them to thaw, they become limp and mushy. This is because all the cell walls are broken and so the liquid juices leak out.

The Romans made ice cream 2,000 years ago, but they didn't have freezers to help them. They used to make the liquid ice cream mixture in a small bowl. They placed the bowl in a larger bowl containing water, snow and ice from a frozen river.

Salt was then added to the water. As the salt dissolved in the water, the temperature of the water dropped by an extra 32°F or more. The ice cream mixture then froze into a solid.

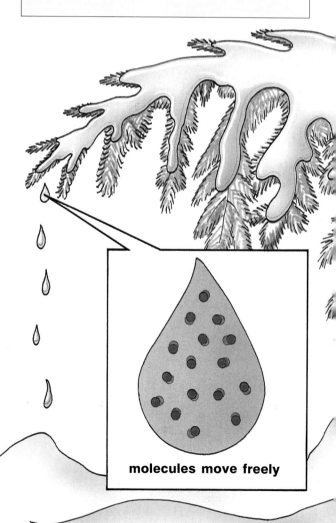

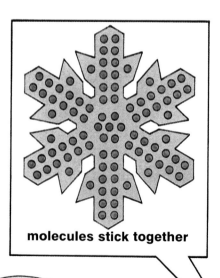

**molecules stick together**

**molecules move freely**

# Banana and chocolate chip ice cream

## Ingredients
1½ cups chilled double cream
2oz finely granulated sugar
1 banana
1 teaspoon vanilla extract
1oz chocolate chips

**Equipment**

food scale
an electric mixer or hand whisk
a bowl
a fork
a plate
a tablespoon
a flat container such as a baking tin
a plastic container with a lid

1 Put the flat container in the freezer or ice box to chill.

2 Pour the cream into the bowl and beat until it thickens. Peel the banana and mash it on the plate.

3 Add the banana, sugar, vanilla extract, and chocolate chips to the cream. Mix gently until all the ingredients are combined.

4 Take the container out of the freezer and pour the mixture into it. Freeze it for about 1½ hours until it begins to harden.

5 Now transfer the ice cream mixture to the bowl. Beat with the whisk or a wooden spoon to break up the crystals of ice.

6 Spoon the mixture into the plastic container. Place it in the freezer for 1 hour to complete the freezing process.

7 Take the ice cream out of the freezer 15 minutes before you want to eat it.

# Getting bigger

A baked loaf of bread is much larger than the lump of wet dough that you put into the oven. When you cut into a loaf of bread, each slice seems to be full of tiny holes. Why do bread and cake mixtures get bigger as they cook?

Bakers add a substance called yeast when they are making dough, and cooks add a substance called baking powder to cake mixtures. Both yeast and baking powder give off tiny bubbles of gas when they are mixed with the flour and other ingredients. These bubbles are then trapped inside the mixtures. During baking, heat makes the gas expand and so the tiny bubbles swell. This makes the bread and cake mixtures rise.

Have you ever found it difficult to open a jar of jelly or honey? Some glass jars have very tight lids that are difficult to unscrew. If adults cannot unscrew a lid, they often hold the jar under a tap of hot running water. The metal lid becomes looser because it expands more than the glass jar.

Liquids expand when heated, but they also become more runny. Molasses and cooking oil are runny when hot, but sticky when they are cool.

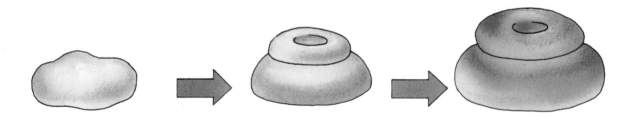

**freshly made dough**          **dough after it has risen**          **baked bread**

Solids, liquids, and gases all expand when heated. The atoms and molecules inside move faster. They push against each other more strongly and try to take up more room.

Before boiling an egg, you should first prick its blunt end with a pin. When the gas inside the egg expands during heating, it can escape through the tiny hole without cracking the eggshell.

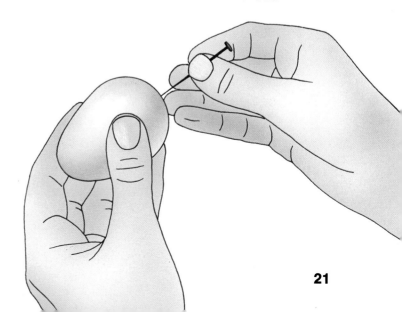

# Wholewheat bread rolls

## Ingredients
1 cup wholewheat flour
1 teaspoon salt
1 package dry active yeast
1 cup warm water
a little vegetable oil

**Equipment**

a cookie sheet
food scale
a large bowl
a teaspoon
a measuring cup
a wooden spoon
a knife
a clean dish towel

**1** Lightly grease the cookie sheet with a small amount of oil. Put the flour into the bowl and add the yeast and salt.

**2** Mix the flour, yeast and salt thoroughly. Make a well in the middle of the mixture and pour in the warm water.

**3** Mix in the water with the wooden spoon. When it is too hard to stir with the spoon, use your hands. The mixture will form a clump of dough.

**4** Sprinkle some flour onto a work surface. Knead the dough with your fists for 3–4 minutes. If the dough is sticky, sprinkle on more flour.

**5** Use the knife to divide the dough into 6 equal pieces. Knead each piece, then shape it into a ball and place on the oiled cookie sheet.

**6** Wet the dish towel and wring it out well until it is just damp. Place it over the rolls and put them in a warm place for about 1 hour.

**7** Ask an adult to help you preheat the oven to 400°F. When the rolls have risen, bake them in the oven for 15 minutes. Leave the rolls to cool for 10 minutes before eating.

# Heat on the move

A pot full of boiling water is dangerously hot, but the pot's handle is cool enough to hold. Pots are made from metals like aluminum, copper, and stainless steel. Metals are good conductors of heat. This means that heat from the stove passes easily into the pot. The handle is usually made from plastic or wood, which are not good conductors of heat. Plastic, wood, and many other solids are insulators. This means that heat does not easily pass through them.

Liquids are poor conductors of heat. Most foods contain a lot of water. If you grill a sausage too quickly, the outside will burn while the inside is still raw. Food cooks as the water slowly conducts heat from the outside to the inside. Gases are insulators, too. A picnic cooler is lined with plastic foam. Gas trapped in the foam conducts heat into the box very slowly, so the food inside will stay cool for a long time.

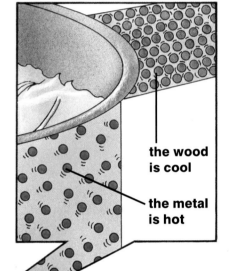

the wood is cool

the metal is hot

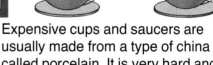

Expensive cups and saucers are usually made from a type of china called porcelain. It is very hard and strong, and it is also an insulator.

Porcelain is made from a special clay and was invented by the Chinese in the 1st century A.D. It came to Europe about 350 years ago, when traders in sailing ships started to bring tea from China. Tea is best drunk when hot, and so the traders brought porcelain cups from China as well. Drinks stay hot in porcelain cups.

# Chinese stir fry

## Ingredients

4 scallions
1 red pepper
2 celery stalks
2oz mushrooms
2 teaspoons cornstarch
3/4 cup water
2 tablespoons soy sauce
1 tablespoon tomato puree
1-2 tablespoons vegetable oil
4oz shelled shrimp

## Equipment

a cutting board
a wok or large frying pan
a knife
a tablespoon
a slotted spoon
a measuring cup
a teaspoon

1  Wash the vegetables. Take the core and seeds out of the pepper. Ask an adult to help you cut the vegetables into 1-inch pieces.

2  Put the cornstarch into the cup and add water to the 3/4-cup mark. Stir well, then add the soy sauce and tomato puree. Stir again to blend.

3  Ask an adult to help you heat the oil in the wok or pan. Cook the onion, pepper, and celery for 3 minutes on a high heat, stirring with the slotted spoon.

4  Add the shrimp and mushrooms and stir fry for 3 minutes. Add the mixture in the cup to the pan (be careful, it might splatter). Keep stirring until bubbling and hot.

# What is convected heat?

The top shelf inside a gas oven is hotter than the shelves lower down. Burning gas heats the air at the bottom of the oven. The hot air expands, takes up more space and rises to the top of the oven. When heat travels with a moving gas or liquid, the movement is called convection.

Convection carries heat through water to the food cooking in a pot. The water at the bottom of the pot becomes hotter. It rises upward, cools, and then sinks slowly downward. As the water moves, it becomes hot all the way through. These movements in heated liquids and gases are called convection currents. They move quite slowly.

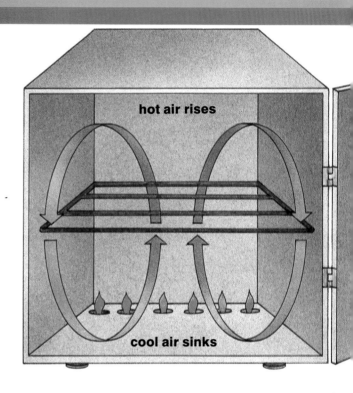

hot air rises

cool air sinks

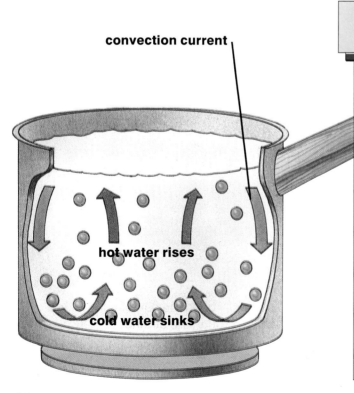

convection current

hot water rises

cold water sinks

Centuries ago, the Maori people in New Zealand did not make pottery, and so they had no leakproof pots or containers in which to boil water over a fire. Instead, they filled a wooden bowl with cold water and placed the food to be cooked in the water. Then they dropped a hot stone to the bottom of the bowl.

The heat from the stone was carried by convection currents up through the water to the food.

# Sea shell salad

## Ingredients
½ cup pasta shells
1 red pepper
1 small onion
a small can of corn
2 tablespoons mayonnaise
1 tablespoon natural yogurt
salt and pepper
fresh parsley

## Equipment

a pot
a colander
a cutting board
a knife
a can opener
a strainer

a large bowl
a small bowl
a fork
a tablespoon
a serving bowl

1 Ask an adult to help you boil a pot of water. When the water is boiling, add the pasta and boil for 10 to 12 minutes. Do not cover with a lid.

2 Drain the cooked pasta through the colander and run cold water over it until cool. Leave the pasta to drain.

3 Wash the pepper and remove the core and seeds. Chop the pepper and onion into small pieces and place in the large bowl.

4 Carefully open the can of corn and drain through the strainer. Throw away the liquid and add the drained corn to the bowl.

**5** Add the pasta to the bowl and mix all the ingredients together with a spoon.

**6** Put the mayonnaise and yogurt in the small bowl. Add the salt and pepper and stir well. Pour the mayonnaise mixture over the salad.

**7** Mix the salad gently so that the dressing covers all the ingredients. Put into the serving bowl and sprinkle with chopped parsley.

# What is radiant heat?

Food cooks quickly when you place it in a hot broiler. But how does the heat move downward from the broiler to the food? It cannot move by convection, which only carries heat upward. It cannot move by conduction, because the air between the broiler and the food is an insulator and so it doesn't carry heat well. A broiler depends on radiant heat to cook the food. Radiant heat travels in straight lines and as fast as light. The sunlight that warms the earth is also radiant heat.

*radiant heat cooks the food in a broiler*

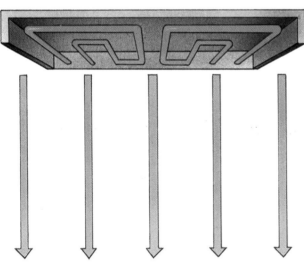

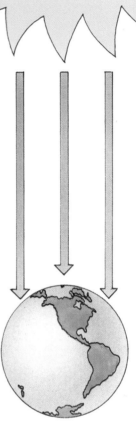

*radiant heat travels from the sun to the earth in straight lines*

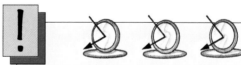

People who live in sunny countries can use sunlight to cook their food outdoors. They use mirrors to catch the radiant heat from the sun. This heat is then directed onto a black metal box that contains the food. Black is the best color for taking in, or absorbing, the radiant heat. The sun's heat then cooks the food inside the box.

Wrap squares of chocolate in pieces of aluminum foil and put them in a bowl of hot water. When the water is cold (after about 3 hours), unwrap the chocolate. Can you explain its new shape?

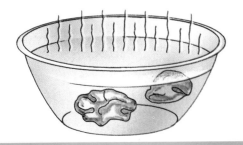

Place a small plum and a grape on a cookie sheet and stand it on a hot radiator for a few days. The result should be a prune and a raisin.

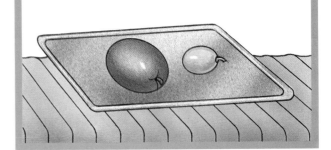

Hold a plastic teaspoon (an insulator) in one hand and a metal teaspoon (a conductor) in the other. Dip both spoons at the same time into a cup of hot tea. Wait for a few moments, and then explain what each spoon feels like.

Take two glass tumblers and place one inside the refrigerator. After 30 minutes, put both tumblers side by side on a table. Breathe into each one. The cold glass becomes cloudier more quickly. The water vapor in your breath condenses more easily on the cold glass.

Fill a heat-resistant glass pot with cold water. Place it on the stove for 5 minutes, without any heat, until the water stops moving. Drop a brightly colored hard candy into the water and warm the pot gently. As the candy dissolves, streams of color appear in the water. They show the movement of the water as convection currents carry the heat through it.

# Glossary

**atom**
The smallest part of any substance. All solids, liquids, and gases are made up from atoms.

**baking powder**
A white powder that gives off a gas when mixed with water. The gas makes cakes rise during cooking.

**boil**
A change that happens to a very hot liquid. Bubbles of gas quickly grow in the liquid, rise to the surface, and burst.

**condense**
A change that happens to a gas or vapor when it is cooled. The result is a liquid.

**conduction**
The way in which heat travels through a solid from a hot part to a cooler part.

**conductor**
A substance that allows heat to flow easily through it. The substance stays still while the heat flows.

**convection**
The way in which liquids or gases move as they carry heat from a warm place to a cooler place.

**convection current**
The movement of a stream of hot gas or liquid that happens during convection.

**crystal**
A small piece of solid with straight sides. All the crystals in a substance have the same shape.

**degree Fahrenheit**
A unit that is used to measure temperature. It is written as °F for short. Many thermometers have a scale marked in degrees Fahrenheit.

**evaporate**
The way in which a liquid slowly changes into a gas or vapor.

**expand**
To get bigger. Solids, liquids, and gases expand when they are heated.

**freeze**
The way in which a liquid changes into a solid when it is cooled.

**gas**
A substance, such as air, that is neither a solid nor a liquid. A gas will escape unless it is kept in a closed container.

**insulator**
A substance that does not allow heat to flow through it.

**liquid**
A substance that is runny and is neither a solid nor a gas. A liquid stays in the bottom of its container.

**melt**
The way in which a solid changes into a liquid when it is heated.

**molecule**
A tiny part that makes up most substances. All the molecules in a substance are the same. Each molecule contains two or more atoms.

**radiant heat**
A kind of heat that travels in a straight line across empty spaces.

**scale**
A row of marks with numbers that is used to measure something.

**solid**
A substance that keeps its shape. Unlike a liquid or a gas, a solid does not flow.

**temperature**
A kind of measurement that shows how hot or cold something is. Thermometers measure temperature, usually in degrees Fahrenheit.

**vapor**
The gas that is given off by all liquids, even when they are not hot enough to boil.

**yeast**
A simple kind of fungus that helps dough to rise. Yeast can be used either fresh or dried.

# Index